Live the Moment
and You Will See and Recognize Yourself

Live the Moment

and You Will See and Recognize Yourself

Gabriele
Publishing House

The Free Universal Spirit
is the teaching of the love for God and neighbor
toward people, nature and animals

Live the Moment
and You Will See and Recognize Yourself

Fourth Edition, October 2021
Published by:
© Gabriele Publishing House
Max-Braun-Str. 2
97828 Marktheidenfeld, Germany

www.gabriele-verlag.com
www.gabriele-publishing-house.com

Tanslated from the original German title:
"Lebe den Augenblick –
und Du siehst und erkennst Dich"

The German edition is the work of reference for all
questions regarding the meaning of the contents

Order No. S 315en
ISBN: 978-3-96446-222-0

All rights reserved

Printed by: KlarDruck GmbH, Marktheidenfeld, Germany

Table of Contents

Foreword..	7
What is the moment?	11
Which law determines our life?	15
We ourselves input our programs	18
Being in oneself or outside of oneself	20
The consequences of the Fall	22
The significance of the night for soul and person	30
Use the chance of the school "Earth" – otherwise your disembodied soul will suffer	38
Become free of self-created causes and of the wheel of reincarnation	44
Every moment is a signpost	49
Our thought-forms	53
The positive energies	60

Our negative thought-forms produce illness, suffering or blows of fate.................... 62

Outside influences 73

Thought-pictures of the past 77

Our pictures of the future 88

Summary 90

Foreword

God is the life, the eternal ocean, the Being.

He is the life of every soul. Once the soul has immersed again into the ocean, God, it has become a mighty droplet of the eternal Being, of the all-encompassing ocean, God, and thus bears in itself all the laws of God; and all the laws of God radiate and act through this droplet. Nothing is concealed from the droplet in God. It bears the All-wisdom and the All-love within, which it unceasingly radiates and passes on! And as it gives, so it receives from the All-might and All-power, God. This is why the droplet is mighty.

The mature soul of our sister is a droplet in the ocean, God. Her soul knows the laws of God and, therefore, all matters pertaining to life, because everything is law. The droplet in the ocean, God, is the opened divine consciousness, the mature, light-filled soul in God. The All-power, God, touched the droplet in God, the soul of our sister, and she began to write what flowed from the droplet in God, from her soul: The truth about the processes that take place in the law of the Eternal and in the law of sowing and reaping flowed from her.

God, the Eternal, sent the spirit being, the soul of our sister, to Earth in the earthly garment, so that she express in human words what human eyes do not see and what human ears do not hear, but which is nevertheless effective. And so, our sister drew from her opened consciousness and put into words what takes place in many people, what happens to them and around them, so that the reader can recognize and change his life and way of thinking — if he wants to. The words in this book are the truth, because they flowed from the truth, from the opened spiritual consciousness of our sister. From this, may many people recognize that they have to change themselves, in order to escape danger and blows of fate.

The dangers that lurk around many people are seldom sensed before the causes become effective. This book, "Live the Moment and You Will See and Recognize Yourself," is therefore given so that people may recognize in time the negativity that is amassing in and around them and waiting to erupt.

The person who strives to live the moment lawfully will recognize many dangers in time, and with Christ's help will counteract the causes, so that they then either dissolve in time, and he no longer has to bear the effects, or he has to expiate only a part of the causes that he created.

Christ, the Redeemer of all souls and human beings, helps and supports every soul and every person.

Ask — and it will be given to you!
Seek — and you will find!
Knock — and it will be opened to you!

The divine world, the heavenly brothers and sisters, greet their brothers and sisters in the earthly garment through me, Brother Emanuel, as I am called on Earth.

I am a servant of God, the Cherub of divine Wisdom, the one responsible in the work of the Lord. I am a being of heaven and am not in the earthly garment. I protect our sister, God's prophetess and emissary, who has drawn what is written in this book from her spiritual consciousness and clothed it in the language of this world.

Peace!
Brother Emanuel

What is the moment?

The moment is a building block of the day. Each moment causes many feelings and thoughts to come up in us. When we examine them closely, they look like pictures: memories of events and experiences or pictures from the world of our imagination.

What radiates toward a person in each moment is what he should recognize and clear up on this day. Each person has a different state of consciousness. The moment approaches him accordingly — with the feelings and thoughts that he can recognize and understand according to his consciousness. Therefore, what the moment brings him is not a "foreign" picture because it is his own former productions.

Thus, what the moments, the day's building blocks, bring to each person are the reproductions of his own productions.

We can also call the pictures that are radiated to us by the day's building blocks, radiation-images. Each moment has as many radiation-images as there are people. Therefore, it can be said that each moment is individual and corresponds to the individual person; for each moment wants to convey to soul and person what the person himself has entered into the mighty causal computer, that is, into the course of the stars, since a person will be controlled by the stars until he has overcome the law of cause and effect.

Every detail of the human ego is stored in this causal computer — all sins, faults and offences. The causal computer consists of the heavenly bodies of the planes of purification and of the material stars. The law of sowing and reaping is stored in these heavenly bodies. They form the wheel of reincarnation.

The causal computer is in the All-computer, because the divine penetrates everything. The All-computer comprises the entire network of information of the universe, the All. It is the law of God, the omnipresent power.

I will go into more detail later about both the causal computer and the All-computer, as well as the pure, fine-material heavenly bodies, through which flows the eternal law, the Absolute Law.

Thus, the moments, the seconds, the minutes, the hours, indeed, the whole day, speak to every single person in his own language.

Each one of us can understand the language of the moment, the day's building blocks — the seconds, minutes and hours — because they are the reproductions of our own productions. The building blocks of the day address each person differently, according to his own productions.

The causal computer again brings out all the human aspects that the person has entered into it in previous incarnations and during this life and that have not yet been cleared up by him. These are all our violations of the eternal law: our negative feelings, thoughts and words, our negative deeds, our passions, compulsions or excessive human desires. It can also be the bindings to our neighbor, from whom we took his freedom, for example, by forcing our opinion on him.

The causal computer brings out as an effect everything that soul and person have not cleared up. Therefore, it speaks to each one of us in our own language! Each one of us can hear in his own language what he has stored and can see in pictures what he has emitted, for they are his own productions. However, we can perceive them only when we live in the moment, indeed, when we live the moment.

However, many people do not grasp the moments of the day. Therefore, they do not recognize the language of their own productions either; they let themselves be driven by forces that are not their own life force. In this way, they become driven people, who let themselves be used by different energies and forces, by souls and energy fields.

Which law determines our life?

We should ask ourselves the following questions:

Why am I a human being? Do I have a task as a human being?

Furthermore, we should ask ourselves: What task do I have? Is there a higher power that assigned it to me? If we believe in a higher power, we should also acknowledge its laws.

Many people know the physical laws of the All, for example, the law of gravity. If we acknowledge this law, the law of the attraction of mass, we should also be able to acknowledge the law of cause and effect as a spiritual law — referred to above as the process of our "productions" and "reproductions." What a person sows is what he will reap.

Our life is the seed. We sow either a lawful or an unlawful behavior.

If we sow and build on the cosmic law of love and All-harmony, on God, we will harvest inner happiness, peace, health, strength and a corresponding quality of life. But if we sow and build on the "flesh," on sin, on the unlawful, we will reap accordingly. Just as we call into the canyon, so does it come back to us.

Therefore, if we sow peace in our feelings, thoughts, words and actions, if we are upright, honest and good, we will reap peace and cosmic power. If we sow discord and condemn our neighbor, if we sow hatred, envy and discord or violate the life in and on the Earth, we will also reap accordingly. Our harvest always corresponds to our sowing.

We should urgently think about ourselves and monitor the subliminal as well — our so-called subcommunications. These are, for example, what we do not express when our words are different from what we think; for our speech can be "sweet" while our thoughts are "sour." The sour thoughts are then our subcommunications.

It is even possible that our thoughts are good, but in our world of feelings, matters may look different; we have a so-called "uneasy feeling," for example. We should pay attention to these deeper stirrings that run behind our thoughts. They are the deeper subcommunications.

Only once we learn to see through ourselves will we find out who we actually are! This requires honesty and a deep belief in a higher power that supports us and helps us to become free from the negativity we still have.

Jesus said: *"Whatever you do to the least of My brothers, you have done to Me!"* Christ is every person's brother. The one who is against another person, his neighbor, is thereby against Christ! He is also against himself, because he himself must reap what he sows.

Whatever a person does to his neighbor in his feelings, thoughts, words and deeds, he always does to himself. This is then his "language" and the language of his harvest as well.

A person's soul is on Earth to purify what he has caused in previous incarnations and in this incarnation and has not cleared up yet.

We ourselves input our programs

The days are the "lesson hours" for every single person. The one who works in these lesson hours conscientiously and also fulfills the tasks — making use of the day with its moments, seconds, minutes and hours — masters the school on Earth, his earthly life. He knows the language of his day and also knows how to interpret it. In this way, he thus finds himself and makes use of the moment. Very gradually, he gets to know the language of his communications and subcommunications. He senses in good time whether what he says also corresponds to his thoughts and also whether what he thinks corresponds to his world of feelings. In this way, he understands himself and is not seized by outside forces that control him.

We enter into the All-computer everything that has no more subcommunications, that is truthful through and through, our positive, selfless being, and it comes back to us accordingly. We are then peaceful, harmonious, honest, sincere, just and kind toward our fellow people. These forces are

God's forces. They help and serve us in every situation. Our life proceeds happily and peacefully — and we are healthy.

However, what we enter into the causal computer likewise comes back to us. This applies to all unlawful deeds, to our derogatory, envious and greedy thoughts, to our insincere, that is, false, words, which may sound sweet, but are actually filled with sourness, disparagement, belittlement, condemnation and envy. We suffer from these our negative productions; for pain, illness or blows of fate are the reproductions of our productions — of the negativity that we have entered in the causal computer.

The fine, selfless feelings, all selfless, positive thoughts, words and deeds, the being for and with our neighbor, our straightforwardness, honesty and justice are the language that the All-computer will attribute to us.

On the other hand, our spiteful feelings, thoughts and words, the disparagement of our fellow people, all our egocentric, dishonest actions and much more are likewise our language, which the causal computer returns to us — and under which we will then suffer.

Being in oneself or outside of oneself

This is why we say: Live the moment and be aware of what the moment wants to say to you!

The person who recognizes the language of the moment and behaves accordingly — that is, who follows or clears up what the moment, the day, shows him — gets to know himself.

Many people do not live the moment and the day, and therefore, do not know themselves. They live either in the past or in the future and do not understand the language of the present.

A large potential of our spiritual and physical energy is where our thoughts are. Then a part of our consciousness is there.

This means that though we may be present physically, we do not live with our consciousness in the present. Therefore, we are split between here and there!

We could also call this a kind of consciousness split. We do not take an active part in the lesson hours of the day, because we are busy with our past or with our fellow people. We notice, for instance, that our neighbor owns this or that, which we cannot afford, or we are occupied at work with our colleagues and think they have been or still are a nuisance to us. And so, we think or speak about matters that do not concern us, or about bygone matters that cannot be pulled back into the present. Or we concern ourselves with the future, although we cannot know for sure whether everything will happen as we imagine it.

My person is here, but my feelings and thoughts are there. This means that I live neither in the moment nor in myself, but outside of myself.

When I'm outside of myself, I am not in myself.

When I'm outside of myself, I open my "house," my physical body, and another one can occupy it; like, for instance, unlawful forces that, by their motives and behavior patterns, correspond to my human ego, to my world of feelings and thoughts. Then they influence me and may even occupy my house.

They direct us quite cleverly by way of our subcommunications, because these correspond to their kind. We hardly notice that we are no longer acting alone, because we do not know ourselves. We are controlled through our own ego, controlled from without, because we were not in ourselves. We opened up our house, our body, because our consciousness, which is our life, was partly outside of us. Many dangers are lurking, influencing those who are not "in themselves," but "outside of themselves."

The consequences of the Fall

The spiritual laws are all-encompassing. We know, for instance, from physics that everything is energy and that no energy is lost. This applies to the spiritual as well as to matter.

Our feelings, thoughts, words, deeds, passions, hatred, envy and discord are energies as well.

A spiritual law says: Like attracts like. It means that like forces attract, in turn, like forces; they combine with each other and thereby reinforce each other. As a result, everything has its field of communication.

Our life runs its course day by day! The day also contains the energy for our life.

Each day can be compared to a powerful stream of energy that brings to each person what is important for him today, in the moment, the second, the minute and the hour.

This stream of energy emanates from the primordial power, the All-power, from God. It is the Absolute Law of love and justice that flows through all of infinity. It flows through all pure beings, the spiritual nature kingdoms and all fine-material stars and planets.

The primordial power flows directly through the pure Being. This also applies to the planes of preparation that vibrate before the gate to heaven.

The souls that are largely purified, that is, beings filled with light for the most part, are located there. They all prepare themselves for the eternal homeland and learn how to apply the Absolute Law in all details. Among them are also such souls that have already frequently lived on the Earth as human beings and have gone through the purification and cleansing process.

All other spheres, for instance, the purification planes and the realms of solid matter, are irradiated only indirectly by the primordial power.

All the planets in these realms contain a part of a spiritual planet, that is, a pure spiritual substance. This is the point of inflow, the switching station for the primordial energy from the All-computer.

For better understanding, I explain in greater detail:

These parts of the spiritual planets — the switching stations for the All-stream — are split-offs from the mighty fine-material planets of heaven. Because of the Fall-event, they were blasted off from these pure ethereal celestial bodies. They serve as switching stations in the more or less condensed planets, the dwelling places of the Fall-beings.

Thus, these parts of the spiritual planets are the "receiving and relay points" for the primordial power. Via these switching stations, the Spirit of God, the eternal law, vivifies the coarse structure that formed around the pure spiritual aspects. These receiving and relay points of the primordial power have enveloped themselves over what for us is unimaginably long periods of time. These envelopments are energies of different rates of vibration. Thus, there are finer envelopments in the purification planes and denser envelopments — the part-material encasements — and the coarse-material ones of solid matter.

I repeat: These encasements, also called envelopments, are the result of the Fall-event.

Since no energy is lost, every bit of energy must be somewhere or other.

Each part of a spiritual planet, the split-off from the pure Being, attracted that frequency that came into its cosmic zone during the course of the Fall-event. This became its magnetic field.

With this magnetic field it then attracted, according to its magnetism, other frequencies, which went out and still go out from the Fall-beings and later, from the human beings. The parts of the spiritual planets enveloped themselves with these frequencies.

The law of sowing and reaping, the causal computer, crystallized out of this mighty Fall-event.

Just as the spiritual split-offs, the planet parts, enveloped themselves with corresponding low-vibrating energies from the negative feelings and actions of the Fall-beings, the same took place with the Fall-beings themselves. In this way, the Fall-planets became mighty causal computers, in which everything is recorded — from the beginning of the Fall-event up until the present day.

Until the formation of the human body, it took innumerable "light cycles," that is, innumerable processes took place in the movement of the heavenly bodies.

As a result of the increasing burdening of the Fall-beings, their spiritual body gradually decreased in size. The envelopment, the condensation, consisted and still consists of the "substance" of their feelings and "deeds." During the further course of condensation to the emergence of the human body, thoughts then came into being.

Since the Fall-beings no longer harmonized with one another, but opposed each other more and more, and since their different desires, longings and emerging passions increasingly separated them from each other in their inner being, the inner communication among them decreased more and more. They developed an external means of communication by using sound. In this way, at the lowest point of the Fall-event, the incarnation shell "human being" very gradually took on form.

At the beginning of the Fall-event, the so-called Fall-worlds first came into being. They assumed a different substance or condensation, depending on how the Fall-beings acted against the eternal law, God. Fall-worlds formed, some out of finer substances, some out of coarser ones. Before the Redeemer-deed of Christ, they were called Fall-planes and afterward, they became levels of evolution. Since the "It is finished," spoken on Golgotha by Jesus, the Christ of God, they separated into planes of preparation and purification planes. Therefore, the Fall-worlds consist of finer envelopments, all the way to the coarsest envelopment — matter.

The purification planes and the solid matter are those realms for all souls and people, who still move within the wheel of reincarnation and are under the radiation of the causal computer.

All development planes up to the pure Being of heaven are levels of consciousness. After the death of the physical body, the soul will, according to its spiritual development, be on that plane, that is, that level of consciousness, which corresponds to its spiritual state of consciousness.

Souls from all levels of consciousness live on solid matter, the Earth. The Earth can be compared to a powerful radar screen that picks up all rays, that is, all souls, from all levels of consciousness.

Because of the very high degree of condensation of the mass Earth, of matter, the suns, the stars and planets can no longer shine through each other, as takes place in the pure Being of heaven, as well as in the planes of preparation and in those purification planes that consist of a finer substance that corresponds to the discarnate souls living there.

Within the material solar system, to which the Earth also belongs, the sun irradiates only those parts of the planets that are facing it. When, by rotating, a part of the Earth turns away from the sun, it becomes dark there; we say, "It is night." Through the alternation of day and night, which benefits both souls and people, the Earth became the greatest place of probation, but also of grace, within the Fall-realms.

The significance of the night for soul and person

The soul in a human being is not of this world. It is a cosmic being of infinity and bears within all the laws of infinity. For this reason, the soul cannot exclusively remain in the physical body for years or even decades, but must, whatever its state of consciousness, be able to spend time and move freely in the cosmos again and again, that is, without a physical body. It can do so when its shell, the person, sleeps deeply. Then the soul leaves its sleeping human body and moves in those spiritual realms that correspond to its state of consciousness. It remains linked to its earthly shell through the silver cord, also called the information cord.

We have already heard about the causal computer and the All-computer.

The All-computer consists of the Primordial Central Sun and the secondary primordial suns, which are the nature and attribute suns, also called the seven prism suns. They disperse the seven basic powers of God, which emanate from the Primordial Central Sun. Each of these seven basic powers is contained in every other one. They radiate as seven times seven powers of the law in the seven times seven pure heavens.

The All-computer is the Absolute Law, God. And what it radiates is, in turn, the eternal All-law, God.

We could also say that the Primordial Central Sun is the origin of the wellspring, God. And what it emanates, the eternal law, is the wellspring, God. The origin of the wellspring and the wellspring itself contain all the lawful principles of God and all the divine information in the All.

The Absolute Law is God.

It took on form in the entity of God-Father. He, the All-One, gave all pure beings the essence of heaven as their heritage, thus granting them divinity. It is the eternal law in which each pure being lives, from which it is and from which it eternally draws.

Thus, the All-computer radiates the Absolute Law.

The causal computer radiates what every single person has entered into it — in the way of unlawful feelings, thoughts, words, deeds, impulses, inclinations, passions, drives or compelling desires — and has not cleared up. All this remains registered in the soul as well as in the causal computer. But when a person repents of his sinful behavior with all his heart and clears it up by making amends, forgiving and asking for forgiveness, then it is erased from his soul.

Therefore, what is remedied in the soul is simultaneously erased in the causal computer. The unlawful energies formerly stored in the computer turn into positive forces, because by clearing up the unlawfulness, the negative is transformed into the positive by the grace of God. The positive then goes into the All-computer and is stored in the spheres of the planes of preparation as a "potential for recognition and memory."

One can say that the soul is also a computer that takes in both the positive and the negative. What the soul absorbs as light is divine and goes into the All-computer; the sinfulness of the soul is stored in the causal computer.

The cosmic law reads: Light attracts, in turn, light; darkness attracts, in turn, darkness.

We should become aware that every aspect of energy is consciousness — whether we call it radiation or power or feeling or thought or word or inclination or action.

The Earth is also made up of innumerable aspects of consciousness. Whether we call them stones, coal, minerals, ores or whatever, all are energies that have their varying degrees of consciousness and radiate according to the vibration of their degree of evolution.

This applies to everything in the whole universe — including soul and person. What the soul radiates as light and shadow also has an effect on the body. The person himself, the envelopment of the soul, likewise consists of countless aspects of consciousness; they are the cellular tissues that also radiate according to their vibration.

So one can say that the person is his thought. He is his body of thought. Just as he thinks and behaves, so does he radiate. This is what characterizes him. The radiation of the soul is its state of consciousness.

All these countless energy aspects are stored in the All-computer if they are positive, that is, divine, or in the causal computer, if they are contrary, that is, negative.

As mentioned before, the soul leaves its material garment at night and goes into those realms that attract it, according to its state of consciousness. There, it gathers different impressions and takes these into its physical body before it awakens the next morning in its "little incarnation." A soul with a higher state of consciousness goes to higher and finer realms. There it participates in spiritual schoolings, which are conducted by pure beings. From them, it learns about God's laws and about the law of sowing and reaping. Aside from this, the awakened and light-filled soul is also given explanations and help for its new day in its physical body. With these instructions, advice and help, it then returns to its body, to its house of flesh and bone.

Upon awakening, the soul is already in its shell, the human being. Via the information cord, it perceives when its body is entering a lighter phase of sleep just before awakening. It has already slipped into its house before the body awakens, or is about to. We notice this when the body jerks upon awakening.

The information, instructions, advice and help that were brought along emanate as radiation from the soul, which is now in its body again. The awakened soul tries to pass on its impressions from the realms beyond matter to its shell, the person, and radiates this wisdom and knowledge into its brain; for precisely these instructions that were brought along by the soul are meaningful as aids for the new day in the earthy garment, both for itself and its shell, the human being.

The person who is aligned with God and lives the moment can receive the soul's impulses and will act accordingly. Especially with the morning impulses, he may already be able to organize his program for the day. If the person then lives the moment in every situation, including his work, he will continuously receive from his soul impulses that it received in the lighter and finer realms.

On the other hand, a soul that is still shadowed and obstinate cannot enter higher or finer realms during the night, because it has not yet opened its consciousness for this. It, too, leaves its sleeping body, but it moves about either in the lower astral realms or on this Earth. And so, the soul takes the impressions back into its body from that place to where it was attracted, according to its thought patterns and correspondences. Such a soul enters its body in a dull and blunt condition, just as its consciousness still is; and then, upon awakening, the body does not really know what to do with its new day.

People who do not use the energy of the day frequently let themselves be driven by various kinds of astral energies, thus wasting their valuable day that also holds many lessons for them. Therefore, the one who let the day pass him by has not taken part in the lessons of the day and has not recognized himself. This means that day after day he continues to build on his causes and therefore, on his fate, on his suffering and on everything that can hit him as an effect.

Therefore, while the physical body, the human being, is deeply asleep, the divine world gives instructions, advice and help for the new day on Earth to those souls that want to be taught. This instruction and help conform to the All-computer or the causal computer, depending on what the stored data will show the person on the new day.

So we can say that our eternal heavenly Father and the pure beings of heaven, our brothers and sisters in the eternal Being, help us in manifold ways. They help us to recognize correctly what the new day will bring us. At the same time, they give us help on how we can clear it up according to the law of inner life. The divine world also helps us to solve problems and to recognize the lawful solution in the situations that the new day brings. However, the prerequisite is that we live the day.

Use the chance of the school "Earth" – otherwise your disembodied soul will suffer

Every person is in the school of life, Earth, and should make use of the lessons, the day! The building blocks of the day, the moments, seconds, minutes and hours, are of the greatest significance for each of us.

Live the moment! Wherever a person goes in his feelings and thoughts, a part of his consciousness goes there; that is also where his mental and physical energy flows, and that is where the content of his feelings and thoughts accumulates.

Let us remember that all souls in the spheres of purification and all the incarnated souls and their shells, the human beings, continuously receive information that corresponds to their state of consciousness. The day speaks to each person in his own language, and therefore, each one can understand the day in his own language as well.

But not everyone can understand another person's language of the day, unless he has stored the same or similar aspect in himself, which is addressed at the same time in him by the All-computer or the causal computer. Then it is possible that two people meet so that they may discuss or clear up with each other what is foreseen for them to do today, that is, now.

I repeat: Everything moves according to immutable laws. As the stars move, so does the causal computer, in which is stored the law of sowing and reaping. It stores all the negativity that was created by a person and radiates back whatever is indicated for that particular day — for every single person and for each soul in the spheres of purification.

The causal computer does not inflict a particular fate upon a person overnight. Over and over again, it admonishes soul and person by way of the eternal law, the All-computer, before what the person himself has entered into the causal computer takes effect.

For example, before an illness breaks out or a blow of fate strikes, soul and person receive many impulses, warnings and hints. The person who lives in the moment perceives these admonitions and warnings.

God, our eternal Father, admonishes and warns us through the causal computer. If a person then clears up with Him in time what he has recognized, then what may have soon befallen him is partly or entirely transformed in his soul. And in the causal computer, it will then be erased in its entirety or partially.

Even when a grave cause is at the root of the problem and the person still has some effects to bear since these serve the further purification of his soul, he can be sure that despite all calamities, if he trusts in God, repents of what he has recognized, asks for forgiveness and forgives, then he will have to bear only a part of the effects of this grave cause. But the one who does not live the moment, and therefore does not recognize or work on his wrongdoing, will have to bear the full effect — then, when the causal computer radiates the whole cause as an effect.

Let us remember: What a human being can clear up on Earth, the soul is often able to do only in long "cycles of light"; for in the spheres of purification, "the clocks run differently." There is neither day nor night, and there are completely different light conditions, so that also the radiation between causal computer and soul runs differently.

When a physical body passes away, the All-computer and the causal computer register this:

What the causal computer stored then comes into effect in the soul at greater intervals, since the causal computer now adjusts itself solely to the "cycles of light." It reflects to the disembodied soul in pictures its causes and the suffering brought on by them. This means that the causes have a much more intense effect on the disembodied soul, since the soul must experience in and on its own soul body the suffering it caused its neighbor.

In the earthly body it would have had the possibility to discard mistakes and sins in the course of days — on the other hand, as a disembodied soul in the spheres of purification, it may be able to do so only in the course of long, unimaginable suffering.

As a human being, the soul could have cleared up many a burden in its physical body; the pain would have been less severe because a great deal of illness and much pain can be relieved by natural healing remedies or pain relievers. In the soul realms, however, there are no soothing remedies; nothing can be alleviated there — for the soul must endure its suffering, which it has inflicted on others, until it recognizes and repents from the heart.

And while the soul in a physical body on Earth receives manifold help from God's hand of grace, in the soul realms it experiences not only pain, similarly as in the physical body, but it also feels the pain and grief of those upon whom it has inflicted suffering, pain, sorrow or worries.

At the same time, it must see and suffer in its soul body the whole scope of consequences of its human ego — including all that it has caused thereby in others.

The causal computer stores the data and brings this into the soul body again as pictures, which bear within pain and suffering. These pictures come alive in detail in the disembodied soul. It feels the sorrow of its own ego in itself and at the same time, the suffering it has caused to others.

The one who thinks about this seriously and becomes aware of it feels addressed by it and will make use of his life on Earth — the moment, the seconds, the minutes, the hours, all the day's building blocks, for these are gifts of grace from God.

The one who lives in these building blocks, in the moments, experiences and gets to know himself and gradually begins to live in the right way.

However, the one who does not live in the moment — because he is preoccupied with useless matters, such as the past or the future, for example, or gets involved in matters that concern only his fellow people — is lived by what he has sent out in feelings, thoughts, words and deeds.

Become free of self-created causes and of the wheel of reincarnation

Thus, the one who lives in the law of sowing and reaping, that is, in sin, is under the influence of the causal computer and will be controlled by it.

We people are called by God, our Father, and by Christ, our Redeemer, to fulfill the laws of God: the Ten Commandments, which are excerpts from the all-encompassing law, God, and the Sermon on the Mount. The one who strives to live accordingly will find his way out of the law of sowing and reaping, which is his own "puddle-law."

A person will continue to live under the pressure of his own causes in the puddle of his negative feelings, thoughts, words and actions, of his passions, cravings and spitefulness until he changes his way of thinking and, with the power of Christ, raises himself out of his own morass. Only then, does he gradually begin to live in God and escape the wheel of reincarnation that is kept in motion by the All-computer.

Only once we have escaped from the wheel of reincarnation by fulfilling God's laws step by step, are we directly guided by God, the Absolute Law. This guidance then takes place from the pure Being, from the omnipresent Spirit of God, without the interposition of the causal computer.

Many people concern themselves with the horoscope, with the influence of the stars on their daily routine. The stars and planets can control our life on Earth only as long as we live under the pressure of our own causes, that is, in those areas where the causal computer is active. However, soul and person can find their way out of the wheel of rebirth through the actualization of God's laws — and then the horoscope is no longer applicable for them, because they are no longer under the influence of the heavenly bodies.

Let us consider the following statement: Purity serves the pure, and impurity, the impure — thus, to each his own: that which he has sown.

The one who moves in purity, in the law of God, has attained rebirth in the Spirit of the Lord. He is at peace with his neighbor and in harmony with the forces of the nature kingdoms, the minerals, plants and animals.

The life, God, is the eternal, omnipresent cosmic law of love and harmony. It flows through infinity and brings about what it is: love, harmony, peace, happiness and health. It contributes to the well-being of the one who lives in the All-law, God.

The eternal law, God, the All-law of love, also manifests itself each day on Earth. It strives to bring to each soul and each person what it is: selfless love, harmony, everlasting happiness and peace.

If a person violates this eternal law of love and All-harmony, he creates his own law, the law of the human ego. It is the non-divine, which the person sows with his human feelings, thoughts, words and deeds. He also sows all aspects of his passions and cravings, of his hostilities and addictions, such as alcoholism, gluttony, excessive sexuality or excessive smoking.

This is, then, his personal law; it is registered simultaneously by his soul and by the causal computer. With it, the soul binds itself to the wheel of reincarnation. Each person creates his own personal law in this way, according to the world of his feelings and thoughts. This is, then, his individual life.

When we think over our life from this point of view, we become aware that what the moment brings us can never be our neighbor's moment, for he has another world of feelings, thoughts and senses. Thus, just as we cannot eat, drink, sleep or walk for others, we cannot live through another person's moment either, and he cannot live through our moment and our situation.

We could very well influence the life of our fellow people by acting upon them, for example, in a domineering way and forcing them to do our will. The very word "domineering" says that wanting to dominate others is an addiction. When we succeed in this, we are bound to our fellow human beings whom we have made servile to us. Every binding is against the divine law of free will. The soul and the causal computer also record such causes.

Therefore, if we have violated the law, God, then the divine eternal law of love and All-harmony cannot directly touch us, because it is overlaid by our personal law, which is also called the ego-law or astral-law.

Nevertheless, the eternal law flows to us: It flows into the causal computer and ensures that what we have caused becomes apparent in our soul and in us, the human being. The divine law thereby works indirectly, via the causal computer, because the superimpositions of our ego-law do not let it flow unhindered.

This means that we have violated the eternal law of love and harmony. We alone are the obstacle that prevents the law of God from flowing directly through us. Thus, it is the causes we created that stand in the way of the divine flow.

Every moment is a signpost

It is therefore of central importance for us to live in the moment, to experience ourselves and to remedy in time what we have recognized as human aspects.

A person who lives in the building blocks of the day, in the moments, the seconds, the minutes and the hours, is guided, and therefore, reminded or admonished in time of what he should implement, so that he does not fall into his own trap and conjure up the fate he himself has entered, the consequences, the effects of his causes. If he does not use the many possibilities, reminders and admonitions, then he will be stricken by what he himself has entered into his soul and into the causal computer. For each day unfolds to each one of us a part of what he himself has input.

At every moment, the feelings and thoughts that concern a person's spiritual and physical situation flash through his mind. They want to either warn him or show him new ways or help him out of a situation or guide him correctly in a situation.

Therefore, the building blocks of life, "the moments," help us to master our life situation. They show us in illness, for example, the way to health. Even if they induce a blow of fate or a disease or illness, we may still be certain that in every blow of fate and in every illness the path to health and freedom is given.

Let us be aware of the fact that the power of God is present in everything, even in illness, fate, suffering and sorrow!

If we turn to God and strive to lead a pure life, we will experience God in the blow of fate, in the illness, in the suffering and in the sorrow and will receive guidance and help in manifold ways and means. God's love and grace are effective when we surrender to Him and strive to repent of the sinful aspects we have recognized, to ask for forgiveness and to forgive and no longer do them.

But if we do not grasp the moments of our life, then they get hold of us and we have to bear what we have sown, that is, what we entered into our soul and into the causal computer.

The "happy-go-lucky" person who lets the day slip by says, "Fate directs us; we have to take it as it comes since it comes from on high."

We should not take things so lightly! We have a mind after all! However, if it is crammed full with all the unessential matters that ordinary people daily concern themselves with, our many feelings and thoughts, then ultimately, we ourselves no longer know who we are, but only that we are called as we are named!

Let us always remember: Our spiritual body, the soul, has been born into a physical body, so that during its lifespan on matter, it may expiate what it has burdened itself with as a human being in former existences and in this existence and has not yet cleared up.

The guide to a higher life, the day, speaks to us and shows us in pictures what we should clear up or what we have already cleared up.

The one who lives the moment is shown by the moment how he can master his situations and his daily work and how he can find his way out of difficulties and problems.

Therefore, the day speaks to every single one of us in manifold ways, according to what we bear within, light or shadow.

Thus, every person is the architect of his fate; for what comes to him has been entered by him into his soul and into the causal computer. Nothing can come toward us that was not entered by us into our soul and into the All-computer or the causal computer. Everything, the positive as well as the negative, is based on our feelings, thoughts, words and deeds, on our impulses and inclinations, on our passions, on envy, hatred or discord. The person imprints himself with the divine and with the sinful.

Just as the wind moves and drives the clouds, in the same way, many people let themselves be driven by their thoughts: from one thought to another, from one situation to another.

We should recognize that the one who lets himself be driven is a driven person, and thus, builds the edifice of his own fate!

Let us realize that everything wants to tell us something!

The one who does not consciously live in the day will be driven. What he has overlooked in the indications, reminders and admonishments of the moment is what will continue to drive him: It is his own ego.

Our thought-forms

If we are not alert and do not live consciously in the day and in the day's occurrences, but outside of it — in the past or in the future — then we waste our life and increasingly lose our physical energy. Then only as much divine energy will flow to us as is necessary to keep the body alive.

Everything else, that is, all other energies, we therefore take either from our fellow people — whom we bind to us like slaves, making them submissive to us and getting them to do our will, or we obtain these energies through addictions such as gluttony, alcoholism or excessive sexuality. However, these additional energies are not pure, but energies that have been transformed down and merely seem to replenish our energy deficiency.

Every addiction indicates a deficiency in the soul. Since soul and person have too little life force, they obtain it through addictions. In the case of such an energy deficiency, the soul as well as the person stagnate in their spiritual development. In many cases, the soul then rebels in order to show its person that he should remedy the deficiencies that led to these excesses and addictions. In this case, too, the building blocks of the day, the moments, are helpful.

Someone who disregards the many hints and admonitions given to him year after year in the innumerable moments of the day creates thought-forms in addition to what the soul already bears.

Therefore, those who stagnate for years and decades, thinking the same and like things over and over again, day after day, create one or more thought-forms — their likenesses, which then stand ready to be called up.

When we think and talk again and again about our past, thus invoking it, so that these images become present in us, we create thought-forms of the past.

When we are at loggerheads with our fellow people for years and repeatedly talk about the reason for the discord, letting it flare up in our feelings and thoughts, we thus create a thought-form.

When we disparage one of our fellow people for years, that is, when we haven't a good word to say about him, we thus create a thought-form.

When we try to put others in a bad light, using any unfair means available, we create thought-forms.

When we slander, despise and ridicule a fellow person or even expose him to others who do so, we create one or several thought-forms.

When we paint mental pictures of the future, regardless of what kind, then we also create thought-forms.

When a person repeatedly ponders over the same or like thing for years and decades, when he talks about them or does the same thing over and over, he creates corresponding thought-forms.

Thus, the one who does not live in the moment for years is not only "out of himself," he also creates invisible thought-forms outside of himself.

To wherever our feelings, thoughts, desires and passions go, a part of our consciousness is there; that is where we build invisible shapes of our human ego.

Let us take note: Everything is energy. Thus, every feeling, every thought, every word, every action, every movement, every passion, every compulsion, every addiction is energy.

Since no energy is lost, it must be somewhere or other. As we know, our positive energies, our divine feeling, thinking, speaking and acting, enter the soul and the mighty All-computer, God. They radiate through the person via the soul and bring about health, peace and happiness in and on us. We then carry these gifts of inner love back into the world and help more people find their way to inner peace and selflessness.

Our negative energies also enter our soul. They are registered by the causal computer.

If we leave unheeded the building blocks of the day, the moments — that is, their innumerable impulses to change our thinking and to fulfill God's law — for years and decades, then we create additional thought-forms. These are ultimately nothing other than our "imprint," that is, we ourselves, because they build up with what we send out as negativity.

We can also call up the thought-forms, which are made up of the same and like aspects of our human ego, our thought-fields.

We can compare thought-forms to invisible, hazy entities that are the pictures of our correspondences, to which we lend the impulses and strength to act through our constantly recurring same or like thoughts.

When we then think in the same or like way as that with which we built up our thought-forms, we give them the signal, so to speak, to approach and influence us. Through our human behavior, we ourselves set in motion our "replicas," our thought-forms, our ego that has taken on form. They come at us like robots and influence or reinforce us to do again what we have built them up with — that, which we ourselves are. They then virtually demand of us to think or do the same or like things again.

These self-created thought-forms build themselves up from our mental and physical energies. This means: The more thought-forms we create, the weaker we become. Our thought-forms do not give us any strength; on the contrary, they demand more and more energy from us, because their goal is that we feel, think, speak or do the same or like negativities over and over again.

We cannot command our thought-forms, the so-called robots, to influence our fellow people. Our thoughts are our own correspondences. They are set in motion by the impulse of a thought or word given by us and do not come at our neighbor, but at us. We have built these thought-forms with our unlawful energies and thus programmed them to ourselves, because like draws to like.

However, one of our neighbors can call up aspects from our thought-forms or draw our thought-forms to himself, so that they also have an effect on him — if the same or like correspondences are present in him or relate to the person who created the thought-forms.

Thus, it can be said that every person who has lived and lives for years and decades outside himself and not in the moment, that is, who does not move in the day, creates his own destructive thought-forms, his robots.

The positive energies

To live in the day means: to correctly accept and take in everything that the day brings, to not let go unheeded the human aspects that it shows us, by recognizing and clearing them up, and to deal with, fulfill and solve the work that lies ahead of us and all else with the power of God.

At the same time, in all that the day brings is contained the answer, the help and the solution. If we live in the moment and ask God for help to master the day in His name, everything that comes toward us today and now — whether it is, for example, personal conversations in the family or at our workplace or our work itself — will run smoothly, because we let the best helper, adviser and friend: the eternal law, God, work in and through us.

Everything is energy. If we imbue our conversations, our work, our thoughts and life with positive energy, that is, with our positive feelings and thoughts, these positive forces will be our best co-workers. They impart life to what we do and show us the shortest way, for instance, to accomplish a work well, or they show us how to carry out a conversation lawfully or to find the solution and answer in a certain text. The positive powers also lead us out of serious situations and show us a lawful way.

Positive, that is, selfless thoughts, are God's forces that repeatedly show us what is positive and lawful.

The one who permeates with positive forces what he does today sets positive forces in motion in a conversation as well as in a workpiece, in a writing, at his workplace, wherever he may be. The positive energies that we have developed through a positive life and that are active in our soul radiate through our soul and through our body and set everything into positive motion. This also results in a positive communication with the workpiece, with the conversation, with the work, with everything that we think and do.

Through a positive, that is, lawful communication, the positive solutions that lead us out of difficulties and situations come up in us, for the Spirit of God is in all things. When we live in the moment, we are linked with Him through our positive thinking, speaking and acting — and we experience God's help in every situation.

To live means to live in God; and this means to live in the moment and to experience and recognize what God wants to tell us. The laws are for each one of us, and not against us. God wants the best for us, and He radiates His love and help to us.

Our negative thought-forms produce illness, suffering or blows of fate

God, our heavenly Father, also wants us to be healthy. If we want to live a healthy life, we must first of all think in a healthy way. Many think that healthy living means eating healthy foods. In so thinking, they often forget healthy feelings and healthy, that is, positive, thoughts.

Let us take the following phrase into our consciousness so as to remember it:

It is not only important to eat healthily, but also to have healthy, that is, God-pleasing feelings and thoughts, and to express and do only what pleases God.

We should not merely talk about health, but also feel and think positively. It is of no use to affirm our health and to talk about health when behind that, in our feelings and thoughts, we fear illness! We must allow ourselves to be completely permeated by positive forces; then they will become active in us and bring about what is good for us.

If we feel and think positively, if we speak of health and live in the moment, we will also choose our food accordingly, because the day's energy tells us via our organs which strengthening substances they need today. They then communicate with us via our senses and our taste buds and show us which food we should give them and how much.

If we live in the day, which begins with the moment, everything that is good for our soul and for our body will be shown to us. Then we will find the seed of the good in everything that comes to us, whether as indisposition or illness, in a conversation or at work. If we build on this, then also what is good for us will develop, because we will tackle and carry out with the positive forces what leads to the good, since we are in league with God, the positive energy.

This applies to every situation in life, whether we are healthy or ill, whether we are hostile or peaceful toward our fellow people, whether we live in difficulties, whether we suffer blows of fate, or whether we live in a carefree manner. The good is in everything! If we find the seed of the good and build on it, things will also go well for us and the negative will gradually transform into the positive, for God helps!

But if we fear illness, worry and suffering, we thus transform down the positive energies into negative ones. As I have already described, by doing this, we create our own destructive thought-forms — those dangerous robots that we ourselves are.

Therefore, let us be aware that danger does not come from without; it comes from ourselves and influences us.

Only what we have in ourselves can hit us. Though many dangers may still lurk in the world, if we do not have the same or like aspects in us, we will not attract these dangers either. They cannot do us any harm, unless we have created a force of attraction for them in our soul.

If we do not reverse in time our same and constantly recurring human ways of thinking, we get caught up in a vortex of our thoughts and can hardly find our way out. This is because our created thought-forms then have an additional influence over us and drive us into a corner, so that we again do and think the same and like unlawfulness.

Let us realize that whatever human aspects we send out influences us again.

Our thought-forms can also prematurely activate causes in our soul, for instance, symptoms of illness that we entered into it through fear and worry. These symptoms that we created and activated then radiate into our body, which becomes afflicted with it. It may be that this symptom of illness would never have affected our body if we had not created additional thought-forms that triggered the illness.

In countless moments, seconds and minutes, that is, on many days, we were warned and admonished to change our thinking. We overlooked the warnings because we did not live in the moment. Thus, what we could have prevented, that is, put a stop to, broke in over us.

We can, for example, give a completely different direction to an ailment or an inflammation through our misbehavior, thus provoking something serious.

If we have had anxious thoughts for years, we can even get cancer. With these thoughts, we created a thought-form that can then affect us, if, for example, in the case of an indisposition or inflammation, we nourish the fear complex "cancer." With this fear that has been nourished for years, we have created a form of energy that we now build up even more with our "fear of cancer." Because of the indisposition in our body, we begin to think again in a same or like way, such as "I hope it's nothing serious! I hope it's not cancer, which I fear so much!" The key word "cancer" now sets in motion our thought-form, in which all our fears of serious illnesses are stored, above all, the fear of cancer.

Since our unlawful thoughts have also been stored in the soul as a correspondence, the thought-form "cancer" now begins to have an effect on us and on the correspondence in the soul as well. We can then only think of cancer. Why? Because the "robot cancer," the thought-form, also influences our brain cells, in which our anxious thoughts about cancer are likewise stored. At the same time, it acts on the correspondence in our soul as well.

These powerful communications between the "robot cancer" and the correspondences in the soul and our brain cells cause the momentary indisposition or inflammation to be "reversed": These negative communications increasingly reduce our spiritual and physical strength and we very gradually create the milieu in which cancer cells can grow. The vibration of our body has meanwhile dropped to such an extent that the milieu is created in which cancer can develop from an indisposition, for instance, from a common cold or an inflammation.

Thus, with our negative thoughts we can cause illness and infirmity in and on our body or conjure up suffering and blows of fate. On the other hand, through positive feeling, thinking, speaking and acting, we bring about health, inner harmony, joy, peace, happiness and contentment in ourselves.

Therefore, we see that thoughts are powers! What we think and the way we think, both come back to us, the sender.

And in this connection, we understand the law of sowing and reaping: "What you sow, you will reap." Expressed differently, every cause has its effect. The cause is the seed; the effect is the fruit.

Thus, we recognize that we alone are the architects of our illness, suffering and blows of fate — and not our fellow people or even God.

Let us remember: If we do not turn back in time, fate will take its course! With our negative, aimless thinking, we can either strengthen or build up again correspondences, that is, burdens in our soul.

Let us bring this to mind in the following example:

A trip by car can, for example, end up in a breakdown, an accident or even a fatal accident. Some rear-end collisions could have resulted in just damaging the car, if one of the drivers had not concerned himself for weeks or months with thoughts of a fatal traffic accident.

The person concerned had not lived in the moment for a long time. The day's energies often warned him to change his way of thinking, like: "Behave differently in traffic! Don't drive up so close, and don't get behind the wheel when you're overtired!" He had probably understood some of these warnings, but had then painted the picture of a car accident in which he saw himself fatally injured. This picture entered his soul.

With this, he created a thought-form or nourished an already existing one that he had produced with similar thoughts a long time before.

A critical situation then developed during a trip. Some cars started to skid, and this resulted in collisions. The shock made that picture of an accident emerge. This picture gave the impulse to the corresponding thought-form. It became active and interfered accordingly. As a result, the driver reacted wrongly and what he had been thinking about for weeks or months occurred! The same or like aspects most likely lay in the soul of the driver; however, they would not have led to a fatal accident if he had not previously created a thought-form. It would have remained with the shock of the rear-end collision. The driver could have thereby recognized with which people, or with which one of the drivers, he should have cleared something up.

Here, too, we see again that thoughts are powers! What we sow, we will reap.

Let us realize that the stronger our energy forms — the thought-forms — become and our own ego builds up, the more helpless we become against them. Our energy flows to where we are thinking. The stronger our thought-forms become, the weaker our body becomes.

I repeat: Our thought-forms take possession of us like robots that have been set in motion; they interfere in the course of our life and in the functions of our body and bring about what we ourselves have built up through our feeling, thinking, speaking and doing.

The day admonishes and teaches us; it gives us hints and solutions:

This could be, for example, encounters with certain people or types of people that awaken in us certain sensations, feelings or thoughts. Or situations and incidents could happen to us, be it in the family or at work. Everything wants to tell us something!

If our work goes well, or not so well, and we are beset by thoughts, the energy of the day wants to convey something to us.

If we then listen carefully to what the moments of the day want to tell us and at the same time, learn to look into our thoughts, that is, to perceive what takes place behind our thoughts, in our so-called subcommunications, then we learn what the moment, the energy of the day, wants to tell us.

At the same time, the recognition contains the strength to solve or do what needs to be done.

If we act accordingly, the negative is transformed into the positive, and the positive becomes stronger in us.

Outside influences

However, if we ignore the day's building blocks, the following can happen:

Our thought-forms become mightier and mightier. They radiate out and connect either with the same or like vibrating energies or they attract souls that have the same or like correspondences as the energies of our thought-forms — thus, ultimately, as the correspondences in our own soul.

These energies or even souls then radiate into our communications via our thought-forms. In this way, an old passion can suddenly, for seemingly inexplicable reasons, reawaken. We then begin again to smoke or drink or overindulge in food, for example.

If we do not heed the first signs, then we give one of our thought-forms the possibility to influence us further. It comes — invisible to us — toward us, and with it, one or several souls.

The impulses from the souls sneak into our communications via one of our wishful thoughts, perhaps in a subcommunication, in which former addictions are still active, because we may have not yet cleared up everything. It is possible, for instance, that a clarifying talk is still necessary with a person whom we offended under the compulsion of our addiction.

Impulses from souls come via these subcommunications. They are the so-called "energy injections" into what we have not yet cleared up. Through these injections of energy, the subcommunication becomes stronger and then appears as a thought; for example, we think, and at the same time feel via our senses, thirst, hunger or the desire for a cigarette.

If we now let ourselves go and give in — not just to drink perhaps a glass of wine or a glass of beer or to eat something spicy or smoke a cigarette, but *really* let ourselves go — then the "chase" begins. The souls drive us to take up former vices, for through our passions and addictions, they satisfy their own cravings that they had indulged in as human beings. Through us, they fulfill what fulfilled them as human beings, and what they have not been able to fulfill as souls until now.

When they find a so-called "fuel pump," they set everything in motion to induce the person to do what they crave for. If the person concerned is not alert, but lets his thoughts wander aimlessly, that is, if he does not make use of the day — and if the same or like thing still lies in him as in the soul or souls that want to use him — then he can become the victim of souls via his thought-forms.

If we do not live in the moment, we are outside of ourselves. We know the expression, "we are beside ourselves." If we are not in our house, someone else can settle in. Let us consider what is stated in Mt. 12:43-45:

When an evil spirit comes out of a person, it goes through arid places seeking rest and does not find it. Then it says, "I will return to the house I left." When it arrives, it finds the house unoccupied, swept clean and put in order.

Then it goes and takes with it seven other spirits more wicked than itself, and they go in and live there. And the final condition of that person is worse than the first. That is how it will be with this wicked generation.

Let us remember: Nothing happens by chance. Nothing that exists is by chance! We are controlled either by the causal law, the causal computer, or by souls — or we are guided by the eternal law, God.

By whom or through what we are controlled or guided, depends on our way of living and thinking.

Selfless guidance comes from God. God, our Father, loves us, His children. We love Him, the great All-One, by fulfilling His eternal law. Then, we are also guided by Him, by God, our Father.

What can harm us when God is for us? Only we can harm ourselves!

God, our eternal Father, supports us in everything and in all situations.

When we daily practice living in the moment, we will recognize the divine guidance ever more precisely; for the Spirit of our eternal Father, who is all in all things, will then help us in everything that comes our way.

He, the great All-One, the omnipresent Spirit, God, is our adviser, helper, protector and leader. He is the answer to all questions and the solution in all difficulties and problems. He helps us find what is lawful in every situation, in everything that comes our way.

If we take these steps toward perfection, toward God, who is our true life, we are and remain happy, joyful and peaceful.

Thought-pictures of the past

When we awaken in the morning, we are placed in this day. Externally, it may look the same for many, since it brings sun, clouds, rain, snow, wind or storm for everyone. But the radiation of the day is different for each individual, just as no person is the same as another one in his inner being. For this reason, the day belongs to each one very personally, because it approaches him personally — above all, according to what lies in his soul, to what he has felt, thought, spoken and how he has acted in the past or present.

If we use the moment, we will experience far less grief, lack of peace and lack of joy.

If despite our efforts and our turning to Christ within us, thoughts of the past keep catching up with us, then we should take a closer look at them. We will then realize that our thoughts of the past are pictures. These show us former situations, impressions and events.

Let us not allow ourselves to be driven into the past or into the future by our thoughts in order to occupy ourselves there with useless things! If, however, such pictures stand vividly before us as if they were present, then it is possible that we did not really live this situation, occurrence or event in the past.

"Did not live" means that we were indeed present as a person in these events, but were not consciously there because our feelings and thoughts — that is, a part of our consciousness which, after all, is our life — were outside the situation. We were too egocentric in our thoughts and were not aware that each moment has something to tell us.

Here are several examples of this:
We repeatedly think about our former home, about our former house, about the furnishings of the house and about various items. In our thought-picture, we see various experiences in this house, with the family or with acquaintances. We see smaller or larger celebrations in the house and in the garden. Why does this picture keep coming to us?

Another thought-picture shows us the nice rooms of our former house, in which items, such as pieces of furniture, carpets or pictures, were of special value. Why?

Another thought-picture shows us situations with our children: Events that we may have experienced, but did not live through, because we were not fully present with our thoughts; nor did we permeate the situations, that is, we did not vivify them. Why did we not consciously permeate them with our presence?

Or in another thought-picture, we are still a child or a growing teenager. What displeased us back then or what did we, in those moments, deliberately ignore? The thought-picture of the past wants to show this to us!

Yet another thought-picture shows us our former garden. Certain flowers, flower beds, trees or bushes appear again before our eyes. Do they want to convey something to us?

In another thought-picture, we are taking a walk with our family or we are on vacation with our partner. When such a thought-picture troubles us: What does it want to tell us? Did we consciously experience that walk or vacation? Was our consciousness, which is our life, completely in the situation, during the walk, on vacation — or were we outside of ourselves in thought?

It may be different thought-pictures that are reflected into the present from totally different segments of life.

Such and similar thought-pictures are triggered by one or more of our thought-forms. It may be thoughts we had back then, in these situations of the past. They detached themselves from the occurrence, and we built them outside ourselves as a thought-form. By way of the causal computer, we are now being reminded through these thought-forms to examine more closely these segments of our life, so that we clear up and bring to a close what entered our soul as a binding or burden.

We may very well have been present as a person in all these past situations and incidents; we may have indeed seen the nice rooms, cared for them or decorated them, moved about in them and enjoyed them. Nevertheless, we did not quite fill with life what we possessed. We extended invitations to smaller or larger parties, personally organized, arranged and prepared everything, and yet, we did not fill the whole thing with life, because we were not present with our thoughts. We were there only physically, but not with the consciousness, which is the life. We may very well have gone for a walk with our family or moved around in the garden; we also enjoyed certain bushes, trees, flower beds and particular flowers; we looked at them and yet were not really present with our world of feelings and thoughts. We even spoke about the beauty of the garden, and yet our feelings and thoughts were not fully there. The body was present, but our world of feelings and thoughts was not in us. We were not in our house, in our body.

If we now feel into these thought-pictures, then it is possible that a feeling of emptiness or of unreality or melancholy comes over us. What does this want to tell us?

Perhaps it wants to tell us that we may very well know that we experienced those situations, but did not consciously live through the moments of those situations. We have experienced and seen those situations of our past with others; however, we did not permeate them with an alert consciousness. We did not live in the moment and did not make use of what the day showed us. All this is indeed already past — and yet it is present.

I repeat:
Our feelings and thoughts are the substance of our life; they are our consciousness. If we are not consciously in a situation, that is, if our consciousness is outside of us, then our body is like a puppet. We carry out what we gave ourselves as a program a long time ago. This then controls us, or we are controlled from without, by other forces — and are thus lived.

Therefore, the past brings pictures into the present and at the same time, shows us via our feelings, for instance, melancholy, joy or suffering, what the pictures want to express.

We can deduce from this that we did not live through certain past segments of our life. We perhaps organized nice parties, put the house in order and placed the pretty objects in the right light. We took care of our family, had good conversations with them, and shared in both joy and sorrow — and yet a part of our consciousness was absent; it was not with us.

What can be done? Those periods of life that we did not permeate with our feelings and thoughts, that is, that we did not properly live through, are now before us and want to be cleared up.

Since there is a solution in everything, there is a solution here, too, so that we can close these chapters of our life today.

We now want to take a closer look at one of these thought-pictures, one that is important for us today.

We let the picture come alive in us; we feel and think our way into it! We now look at all the details that the thought-picture reflects to us.

With our feelings and sensations we now put ourselves into the picture and live through the "glimpses" of our past. We move in that situation and now live through the picture.

After about ten minutes, because we should not revive the past for much longer, we ask ourselves critically whether what we have now recognized is still important for us today. Or what if back then we had lived through and shaped those situations that are still present in us? Or: What would the present look like, if we had been open-minded, accessible, understanding and helpful back then? Or: What would have become of it, if we had lived through the situation then, that is, if we had lived the moment consciously? We now let all of this come to us.

If we have permeated the picture with our world of feelings, sensations and thoughts and perhaps even physically felt what we could not experience back then, for instance, joy, sorrow, pain, suffering or love; and if we have weighed the pros and cons with an honest heart, then we can recognize whether we should forgive people or ask for forgiveness or make amends for something. We should then do this and not postpone it. Or we can even discard a few pictures or situations right away, so that these now enter our world of memory.

In this way, one segment of life after another enters the realm of our memories. That is, we may well still remember the various segments of our past, but we are no longer attached to them, and they no longer preoccupy us.

The same procedure helps us when hostilities from the past still exist:

Let us also experience ourselves in such a picture and allow it to come alive!

If we are willing to close the past, we will also see ourselves and the seemingly guilty person in this thought-picture, and will be able to remedy all that has led to the quarreling and enmity.

But let's take a closer look! Was only the other one the culprit, or weren't we also involved? No "buts" please! Let's look more closely! No dispute is one-sided; it always takes two to quarrel. The following question can help us recognize ourselves: What was there in us, in me, at the moment the quarrel broke out?

The one who looks deeper keeps the eternal laws!

Have we become more alert and aware by looking into the picture? If yes, we will take the first step and ask our neighbor or neighbors for forgiveness.

If in this way we saw our wasted moments and our past as if in fast motion and revived them by putting ourselves in them, then it is possible for us to close the past and turn to the present and higher life.

The closed pictures of the past go back into the consciousness layers between the conscious mind and the subconscious, where our memories are stored.

When we revive such pictures from the past, we should always do this with the inner intention of transforming the still vibrating programs with the light of Christ. We should not let the past come up again out of curiosity, or even "rummage about" in it with our thoughts, but let it "come to life" in us only when the energy of the day gives us such a picture so that we may clear something up.

Our pictures of the future

Pictures of the future can become even more dangerous for us than the past that we did not live through.

If we are not willing to live in the moment, we tend to escape into pictures of the future. For example, we envision passionate scenes or make up heroic roles for ourselves; we plan exactly how everything has to run in order to achieve what we build up in our imaginary world — we build "castles in the air." All this becomes thought-forms.

When something comes up today from the burdens of our soul so that we clear it up today, this can also become a picture of the future, namely, if we postpone it and instead of clearing it up, continue to reinforce it with negative thoughts and actions and project it into the future.

We think, for example: "If I don't manage it today, I'll manage it later." So we are not living in the moment, but in the future, thus creating a thought-form!

But what use are our pictures of the future? Do we know if it will come as we wish or imagine it?

On the other hand, however, we can and should plan our future conscientiously. Then we should place our plan in the will of God and leave it with God. When we then live in the moment, God can guide us; and we will recognize whether what we planned is also good for us.

However, we should not want to stubbornly insist on something that wants to take another path! Who knows whether it isn't better for us in the way it wants to go? He alone knows, who knows all things — the Inner Helper and Adviser, God.

If we create pictures of the future as thought-forms, these also influence us when we call them up with the same or like thoughts with which we created them. They have an effect on us and try to push us in the direction that we entered into them.

If we are not alert, that is, if we do not live in the moment, they will lead us past the real tasks of our life on Earth, and we will no longer come to know what was given to us to clear up or fulfill during this earthly existence. Then we do not live, but are lived. We are puppets of our thought-forms and possibly of those souls that have settled into these thought-forms.

Summary

I would like to summarize the essential points once more.

Each day brings to every person what is waiting to be cleared up or fulfilled by him on that day.

The days show themselves in individual situations, in occurrences, in conversations, through feelings and thoughts, in words and actions. The day also shows itself through our fellow people, colleagues, relatives, acquaintances, and through the members of our family. The alert person who lives the moment can read a great deal from it and set the right course for the rest of his life.

The one who does not live in the building blocks of the day creates more and more thought-forms, that is, robots, to which he is bound, because they are a part of him.

Since the thought-forms belong to the person who created them, they are connected to the causal computer, just like the person and the soul of the person.

The robots with their many-sided inputs then approach us and influence us, if we call them with the same or like thoughts with which we formed them.

Those who do not live in the moment, in the day, are lived and therefore cannot see in the right light the situations of the day and all that it brings, and find the solution.

And when we move around in the day's occurrences and our feelings and thoughts are not with our work, with the situation, that is, they are not in the moment, we do not permeate with life what the day brings; instead, a part of our consciousness is at that place where we are in our feelings and thoughts. This means that we do not live in the present but, for example, in the past or in the future.

The day then takes with it again what we have not accepted and cleared up today, and brings it back another time. But it can be that what it wanted to show us today will come to us tomorrow, the day after tomorrow or after years, in a far more intense and burdening way, because meanwhile, we have continued to build on it with the same or like feelings and thoughts.

What the day then takes with it again is thus not remedied, but simply postponed.

Many of the day's impulses admonish and warn us. If we repeatedly let the admonishments and warnings pass us by, then what the day has indicated and what it drew our attention to, so that we clear it up, will one day come to us powerfully and interfere in our life: either through a blow of fate or through illness and suffering.

When the day then comes that brings the demise of our body — which is unavoidable, since death does not demand any decision from us, because it directly enters our physical body — then we as a soul take with us into the purification planes what the days brought us and we left unheeded. Then it is even possible that we take considerably more burdens with us into the worlds beyond than we had brought with us when we entered this earthly existence; for what we have not grasped has continued to grasp us. Thus, we have added more to the already existing faults and sins and even built on them.

When in the causal computer there is no indication of a further incarnation, our soul takes our thought-forms with it as burdens. The soul will then dissolve these shadows during its further maturing process.

However, if we have set the wheel of reincarnation into motion again for our soul by continuing to burden ourselves on Earth, then some thought-forms will remain in the Earth's atmosphere when our physical body passes away. If our soul slips once more into a newborn physical body, our deposited thought-forms will then come to us when we as human beings have the maturity to distinguish good from evil. If now the causal computer stimulates the correspondences of our soul and the day wants to point them out to us, but we do not heed them — just as in our previous incarnations — then we call up from the atmosphere the thought-forms we deposited there in a former life. They come toward us and reinforce our unlawful way of thinking, speaking and acting — all that we should have overcome with the power of Christ!

Everything human, that is, everything unlawful that has not been atoned for or cleared up, will keep coming toward us — either toward the soul in the soul realms or toward the human being on Earth — until we remedy it all through remorse, by asking for forgiveness, making amends and then no longer doing it.

Let us remember that the law of cause and effect brings everything to light! Thus, we can also better understand the statement: God's mills grind slowly.

We feel what we have not cleared up, our sins, in and on our body as pain, illness, suffering or a blow of fate. In the soul realms, we feel directly in and on our soul body what we have done to our neighbor — and be it only in thoughts. As a soul we feel the pain, the suffering and everything that our neighbor felt and suffered because of our behavior. In some cases, this can be the so-called torments of hell for our soul!

Our soul also has to atone for the following: Due to our human, egocentric behavior, our neighbors got into situations that were not intended for them in this incarnation, and from which they could not find their way out in time, and as a result, their lives took a completely different turn.

Or: If we force our neighbors to do this or that, or if we even threaten them and use methods to obtain what we want for ourselves, then we are bound to these neighbors and must feel, experience and suffer everything in and on our soul body: their annoyance, their resignation and not least, also what they could not overcome in their earthly existence, because we interfered in the course of their life. Everything that our neighbors could have experienced and cleared up during their life on Earth, we have to expiate and suffer through with them.

And the one who does under compulsion what his neighbor demands from him binds himself as well to the one who makes these demands. Both — the one who demands and the one who lets himself be subjugated — are bound to one another. They will be brought together again and again, whether in this incarnation, in further incarnations or in the soul realms, until what has bound them to one another is remedied.

Therefore, let us recognize that a moment that has gone by unheeded can trigger an avalanche of dangers.

This is why the statement "live the moment and make use of your time on Earth so that as a soul you will live in more light-filled and finer spheres" is of great significance.

Every person dies. At the moment of the birth of our physical body, physical death is already predetermined. Unlawful forces will not use the person who makes use of the time from that moment in which he is able to differentiate between good and evil. He will hardly create any thought-forms, because he is himself and grows into the true Being — into the divine Self, into freedom, which is the spiritual birth of the soul.

Therefore, live the moment — and you will recognize yourself and find the way into the impersonal, into your divine Self! You will then experience who you are, and who and what your true Self is.

May everyone who reads this book recognize the grace of God!

It is never too late if from now on we turn back immediately and, with Christ's help, make use of the moment and remedy or fulfill what we have recognized today. Then we no longer give nourishment to our ego, and our thought-forms also transform into positive energies, because Christ in God, our Father, transforms everything and makes everything new, if we let ourselves be led by Him.

Read also:

The Path of Forgetting
The Microcosm in the Macrocosm

The explanations given in this book tell us that everything that we as human beings feel, think, speak and do, not only is unceasingly recorded in the microcosm "human being" but is also in constant communication with further memory sources in the coarse-material macrocosm and, beyond that, in a finer-material macrocosm.

Whoever not only reads the contents but thinks about it and relates it to everything that he encouters at every moment, will find that new knowledge opens up to him, the far-reaching significance of which is unspeakably valuable for shaping his life.

112 pp., SB, ISBN 978-3-89201-807-0
Also available in eBook form

The Soul
on Its Path to Perfection

Through Gabriele, the prophetess and emissary of God in our time, the Christ of God reveals details on the structure of creation of the eternal Being and of our soul. Christ extensively explains the seven levels of consciousness of the soul – from Order via Will to Wisdom, then Earnestness up to Patience, Love and Mercy.

To activate these soul-levels is the task of each soul – here on Earth or in the spheres of the beyond. We also receive answers to many questions: What does the soul have to recognize and learn on the individual levels? What is it like for a soul that leaves its physical body in young years? And much more ...

116 pp., HB, ISBN 978-3-89201-952-7
Also available in eBook form

This Is My Word
A and Ω

The Gospel of Jesus
The Christ-Revelation
which true Christians the world
over have come to know

Building on the "Gospel of Jesus," an existing extra-biblical gospel text, Christ, Himself, explain, corrects and deepens the facts about His life and teachings as Jesus of Nazareth via Gabriele, the prophetess and emissary of God in our time. Learn that Jesus never founded religions. He installed no priests or pastors and taught no dogmas, rituals or cults. 2000 years ago, Jesus brought the truth from the Kingdom of God: The teaching of the love for God and neighbor toward people, nature and animals; the teaching of freedom, of peace and of unity. He spoke about the God of love, about the Free Spirit – God in us.

From the contents: Childhood and youth of Jesus • The falsification of the teachings of Jesus of Nazareth in the past 2000 years • Meaning and purpose of life on Earth • Jesus taught the law of cause and effect • Prerequisites for healing the body • Jesus taught about marriage • The Sermon on the Mount • On the nature of God • God is not a wrathful God of vengeance • The teaching of "eternal damnation" is a mockery of God • Jesus exposed the scribes and Pharisees as hypocrites • Jesus loved the animals and always championed them • On death, reincarnation and life • The true meaning of the Redeemer deed of Christ ... and much more.

A short autobiography of Gabriele,
the prophetess and emissary of God is included
as well as a charcoal drawing

1078 pp., SB, ISBN 978-1-890841-38-6
Also available in eBook form

We will be happy to send you free of charge
the current catalog of our books as well as the many
free excerpts to various topics.

Gabriele Publishing House – The Word

North America: P.O. Box 2221, Deering, NH 03244
Toll-free Order No. 1-844- 576-0937

Germany: Max-Braun-Str. 02, 97828 Marktheidenfeld
International Orders: +49.(0) 9391-504-843

www.gabriele-publishing-house.com